NATALIE MERCHANT
OPHELIA

Piano/Vocal Arrangements by John Nicholas, Todd Lowry and Donald Sosin

Photography by Mark Seliger and Peggy Sirota

ISBN 1-57560-207-5

Copyright © 1999 Cherry Lane Music Company
International Copyright Secured   All Rights Reserved

The music, text, design and graphics in this publication are protected by copyright law.
Any duplication or transmission, by any means, electronic, mechanical, photocopying, recording or otherwise, is an infringement of copyright.

Visit our website at www.cherrylane.com

© Peggy Sirota

The song *Effigy* has been intentionally omitted.

© Peggy Sirota

© Peggy Sirota

Ophelia

Words and Music by
Natalie Merchant

Copyright © 1998 Indian Love Bride Music (ASCAP)
International Copyright Secured   All Rights Reserved

Cur - va - ceous thighs, vi - va - cious eyes,

love was at first sight. Love was at first sight.

Love.

O -

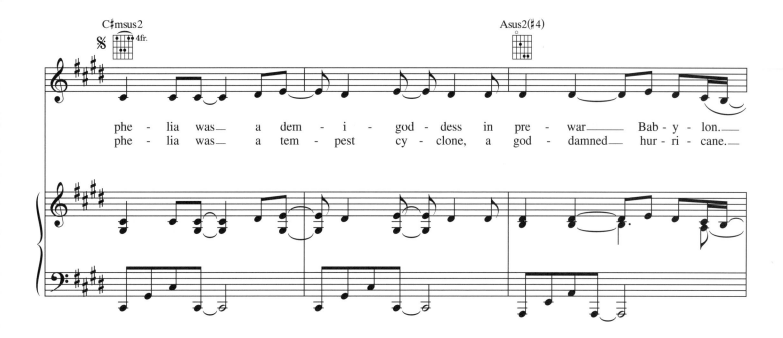

phe - lia was— a dem - i - god - dess in pre - war— Bab - y - lon.—
phe - lia was— a tem - pest cy - clone, a god - damned— hur - ri - cane.—

So stat - u - esque,— a sil - hou - ette— in
Your com - mon sense,— your best de - fense— lay

black sat - in eve - ning gowns.— O - phe - lia was the
wast - ed and in vain.— For O - phe - lia'd know— your—

mis - tress to_____ a Ve - gas gam - bling man._____ Si -
ev-'ry woe___ and ev-'ry pain you'd ev - er had._____ She'd

gno - ra O - phe - lia Mar - a - schi - na. Ma - fi - a cour - te - san.___
sym - pa - thize___ and dry your eyes___ and help you to for - get,___

O - phe - lia was the cir - cus queen,___ the

Life Is Sweet

Words and Music by
Natalie Merchant

Moderately

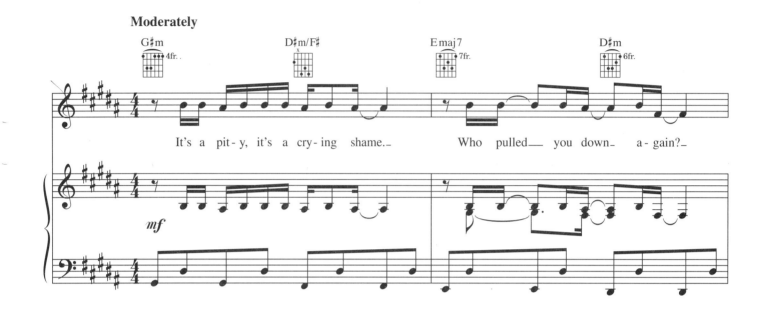

It's a pit-y, it's a cry-ing shame. Who pulled____ you down____ a-gain?____

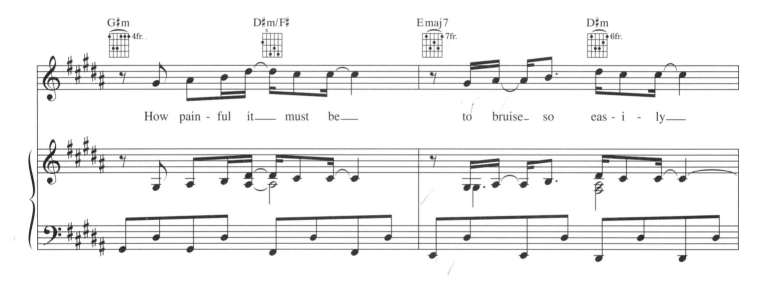

How pain-ful it____ must be____ to bruise____ so eas-i-ly____

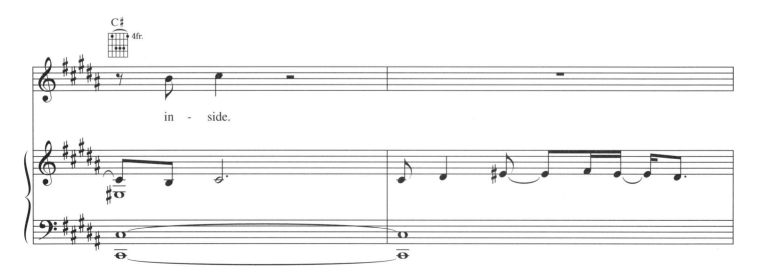

in - side.

Copyright © 1998 Indian Love Bride Music (ASCAP)
International Copyright Secured   All Rights Reserved

I tell you life is sweet in spite of the mis-er-y. There's
I tell you life is short. Be thank-ful be-cause be-fore you

so much more, be grate-ful.
know it, it will be o-

Well,
So

who do you be - lieve?
who will you be - lieve?

Who will you lis-ten to, who will it be? Be-cause it's high time that you de-

Your dad-dy the war__ ma-chine,__ and your ma-ma the long and suf-fer - ing, pris - 'ner_____ of what _____ she can - not_____ see.

D.S. al Coda I

2. For they__

Kind & Generous

Words and Music by
Natalie Merchant

Moderately

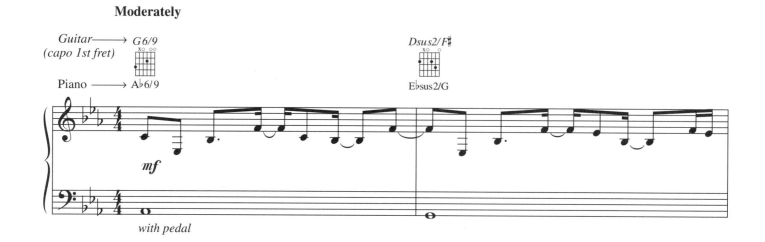

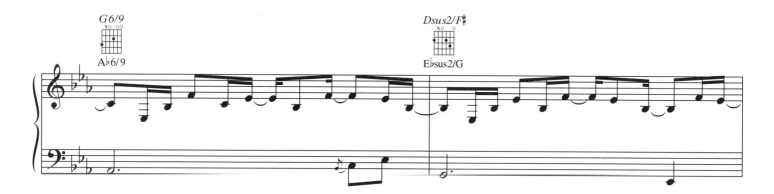

Copyright © 1998 Indian Love Bride Music (ASCAP)
International Copyright Secured All Rights Reserved

Na na na na na na na na na na na na na na na na na,

na na na na na, na na na na na na,

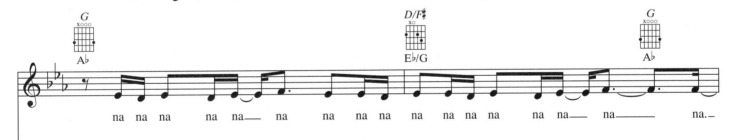

na na na na na na na na na na na na na na na na.

Mm.

Frozen Charlotte

Words and Music by
Natalie Merchant

Blue— like the win - ter snow— in this full moon,—
Still— as the riv - er grows— in De - cem - ber,——

*Recorded a half step lower

Copyright © 1998 Indian Love Bride Music (ASCAP)
International Copyright Secured   All Rights Reserved

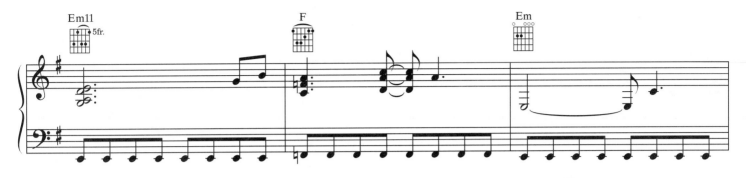

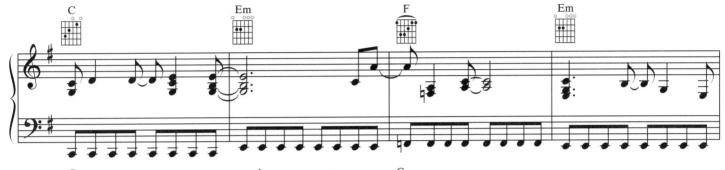

D.S. (take 2nd ending) al Coda

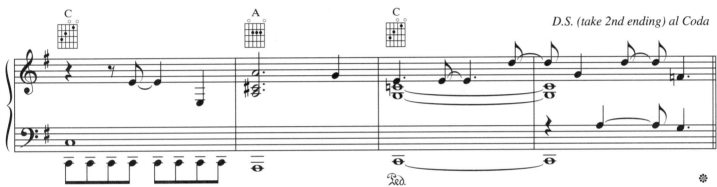

Coda

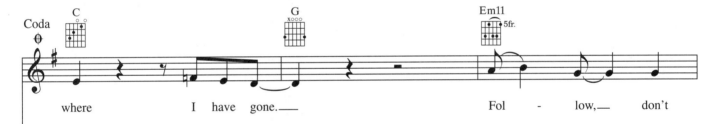

where   I have gone.__   Fol - low,__   don't

fol - low   me__   to where   I've   gone.__

Some - day___ you'll take my place,___ and I'll___ wait

for___ you___ here.

My Skin

Words and Music by
Natalie Merchant

Moderately

Copyright © 1998 Indian Love Bride Music (ASCAP)
International Copyright Secured   All Rights Reserved

sad - ness, the weak - ness. Oh, I need— this. I need a

lull - a - by, a kiss good - night, an - gel, sweet love of my life.— Oh, I

need this. I'm the slow dy - ing flower,— frost kill - ing hour, the

sweet turn - ing sour and un - touch - a - ble. Do you re -

mem - ber the way that you touched me be - fore, all the trem - bl - ing sweet - ness I

loved and a - dored? Your face sav - ing prom - i - ses whis - pered like prayers, I don't

need them. I need the dark - ness, the sweet - ness, the
dark e - nough? Can you see me? Do you

sad - ness, the weak - ness. Oh, I need____ this. I need a
want me? Can you reach me? Or I'm leav - in'. You bet - ter

Break Your Heart

Words and Music by
Natalie Merchant

*Recorded a half step lower.

Copyright © 1998 Indian Love Bride Music (ASCAP)
International Copyright Secured   All Rights Reserved

ooh, oh.

Moderately, with a beat

Peo- ple down-cast in__ de- spair,_ see the dis- il- lu- sion ev- 'ry- where,_
Peo- ple shal- low, self - ab- sorbed,_ see the push and shove_ for their_ re- wards._ When

hop- ing their_ bad luck_ will change;____ gets a lit- tle hard- er ev-
"I, me, my" is on_ their minds,____ you can read a- bout_ it in_

'ry day._
_ their eyes._

way things are, and the way they've been,
way things are, and the way they've been.

1.

and the way they've al - ways been.

2.

Yeah, I know that it will hurt

Yeah, I know that it___ will hurt___

own life.___ And don't dis - re - spect___ your - self;___

don't lose your pride. And don't think ev-'ry-bod-y's got-ta

choose a side. Oh no (oh no),

oh no, oh no,

Repeat and fade

no.

King of May

Words and Music by
Natalie Merchant

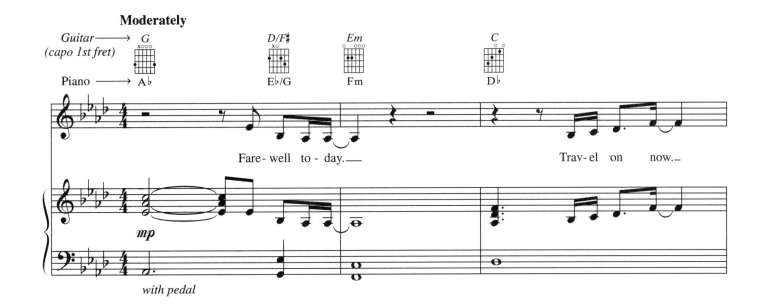

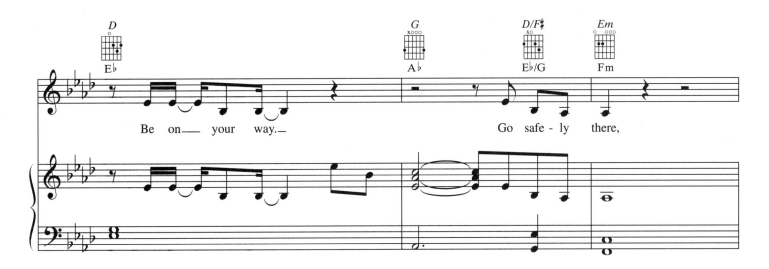

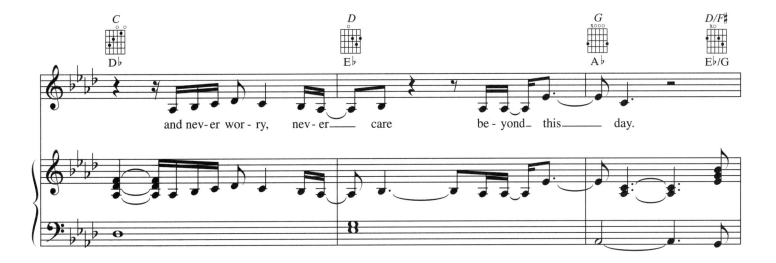

Copyright © 1998 Indian Love Bride Music (ASCAP)
International Copyright Secured   All Rights Reserved

Make read - y for the last__ King of May.
Make read - y for the last__ King of May.

Make a card - board__ crown__

__ for him, and make your voic - es one,__ praise a cra - zy moth-

er's son who loved__ his__ life.

Make a hole in the crowd__

Thick as Thieves

Words and Music by
Natalie Merchant

Copyright © 1998 Indian Love Bride Music (ASCAP)
International Copyright Secured   All Rights Reserved

dared to bite___ the hand___ that fed us. Fair- y tale, the mor - al end.___

Wheel of for - tune nev - er turns a - gain,___

nev- er turns___

___ a - gain.

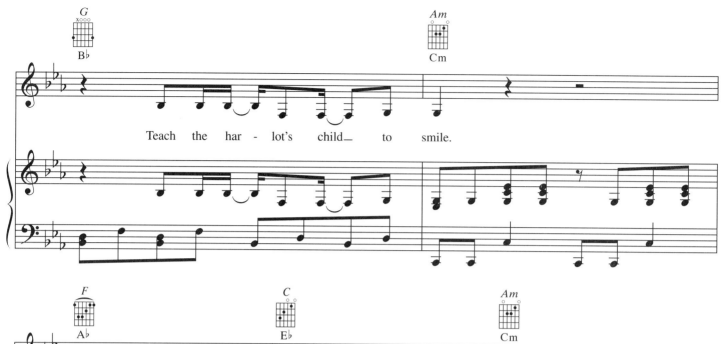

Teach the har - lot's child— to smile.

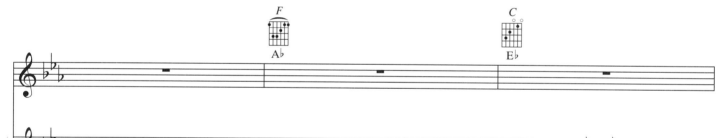

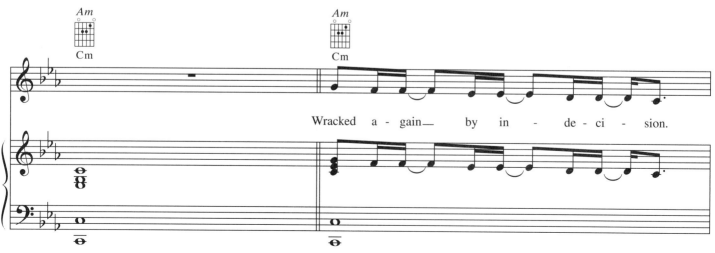

Wracked a - gain— by in - de - ci - sion.

Deep and black,_____ smoke and ash._

The

wick-ed king_ of par-o-dy_____ is kiss-ing all_ his en-e-mies on the

64

I've

come to-night,— and I've come to know— the way— we are,— the way— we'll go and to

meas-ure this, the width of the wide a-byss.— I

come to you— in rest-less sleep,— where all— your dreams turn bit-ter-sweet, with

voo-doo doll phi-los-o-phies, day-glow ho-ly trin-i-ties. The

at   last.

Repeat and fade

The Living

Words and Music by
Natalie Merchant

Copyright © 1998 Indian Love Bride Music (ASCAP)
International Copyright Secured   All Rights Reserved

side— with the liv - ing,— with the liv - ing?—

In a fall - en down place I can hide— from— the

liv - ing,— from— the liv - ing.— 'Cause I don't care to stay—

with— the liv - ing.—

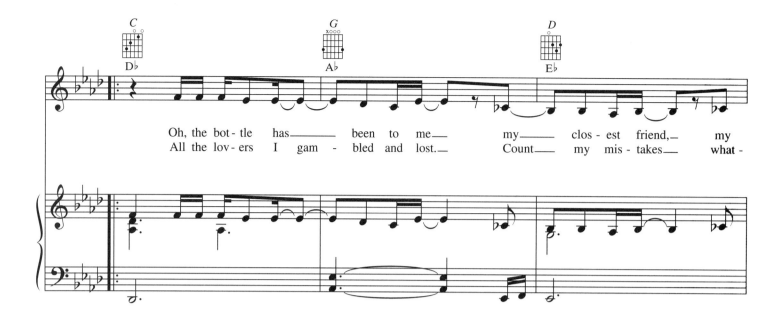

Oh, the bot-tle has____ been to me____ my____ clos-est friend,____ my
All the lov-ers I gam - bled and lost.____ Count____ my mis-takes____ what -

worst en - e - my.____ A - fraid that I walked a fine line,____
ev - er the cost.____ I'll go off, I'll make my - self scarce.____

squan - dered it all____ and wast - ed my time.____ And I don't stand a chance____
Ooh, come to-mor - row you won't find me here.____ 'Cause I don't care to stay____

When They Ring the Golden Bells

Dion de Marbelle (1887)
Arranged by Natalie Merchant

*Sing harmony 3rd time
only (next 7 bars).

Copyright © 1998 Indian Love Bride Music (ASCAP)
International Copyright Secured All Rights Reserved

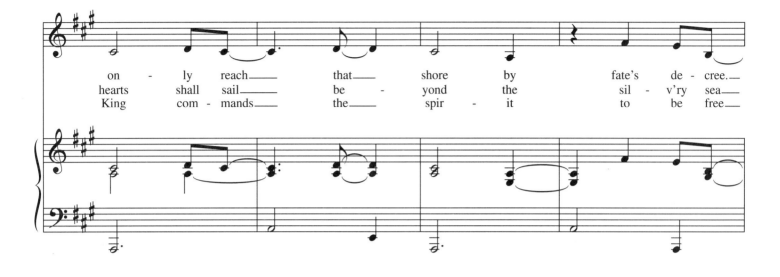

on - ly reach____ that____ shore by fate's de - cree.
hearts shall sail____ be - yond the sil - v'ry sea____
King com - mands____ the____ spir - it to be free____

E   Esus4   E

*
____
____ (sea)._____
____ (free)._____

One   by
We   shall
Nev - er -

*Sing harmony 2nd and 3rd
times only (next 7 bars).

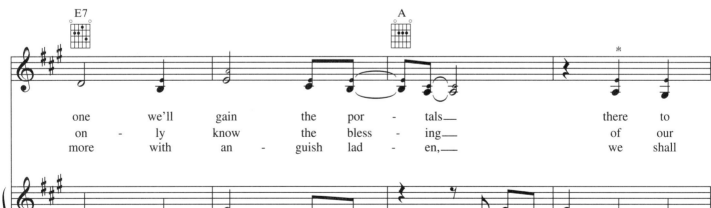

E7   A
                                          *
one   we'll   gain   the   por - tals____   there   to
on - ly   know   the   bless - ing____   of   our
more   with   an - guish   lad - en,   we   shall

*Sing harmony
all three times.

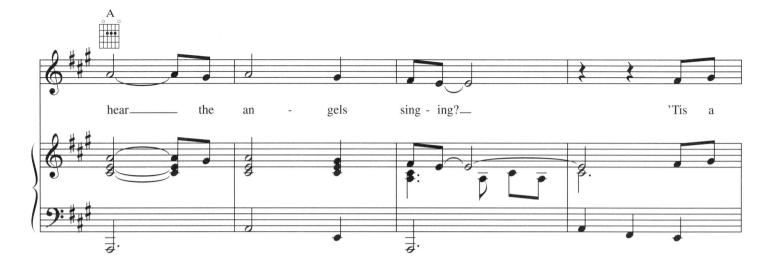

hear_____ the an - gels sing - ing?___ 'Tis a

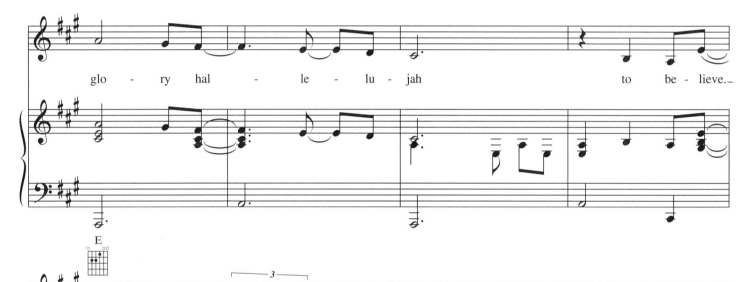

glo - ry hal - le - lu - jah to be - lieve.___

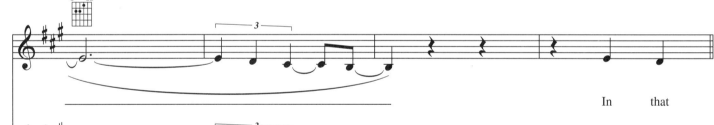

In that

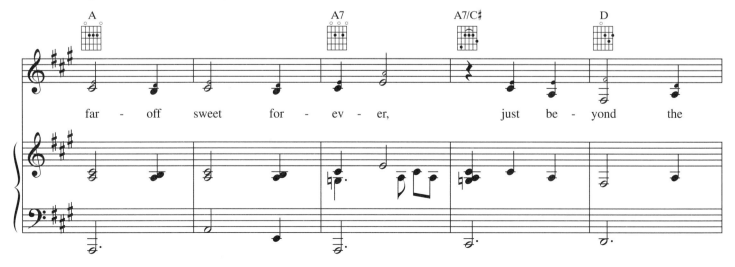

far - off sweet for - ev - er, just be - yond the